ESPIONAGE BLACK BOOK ONE

ESPIONAGE BLACK BOOK ONE:
Intelligence Databases Explained

Henry W. Prunckun

Bibliologica Press

Acknowledgements
Appreciation to Dr Marcus Gossler for the photograph in figure 2,
Ianaré Sévi of Lorien Technologies for the photograph in figure 3,
and Skwanem for the photograph in figure 4.

Espionage Black Book One:
Intelligence Databases Explained

ISBN 978-0-6485093-8-7

NATIONAL
LIBRARY
OF AUSTRALIA

A catalogue record for this
book is available from the
National Library of Australia

Bibliologica Press
P.O. Box 656
Unley, South Australia, 5061
Australia

CONTENTS

CHAPTER ONE
INTELLIGENCE DEFINED

OVERVIEW

Intelligence is a word that conjures assorted notions of spying and espionage, secrets, and the world of covert gadgetry. Yet to some people, the word *intelligence* is closely associated with the Orwellian concept of "Big Brother"—a world of hard-ball politics and an uncompromising quest for power and influence.

There is no doubt that intelligence work is associated with all these concepts. But as will be explained, intelligence in its lowest common denominator is no more than the use of sound qualitative and quantitative research methods. To support secret research, the intelligence database was created.

This book discusses the construction of databases for secret research, but not the spreadsheet-type analytical technique used by researchers to perform statistical calculations once their research-in-chief is complete.

In the classic text on strategy—*The Art of War*—Sun Tzu posited that decisions that were not based on knowledge are an inefficient use of resources and potentially dangerous.[1]

So, the potential power of information is well known and universally recognized. Yet how do intelligence analysts construct these databases? What is the logic behind their structure? This book explains these issues and discusses other matters relating to the construction of intelligence systems. In this way, readers can better understand intelligence databases.

---

1. Sun Tzu, *The Art of War*, translated by J. Clavell (New York, NY: Delacorte Press, 1983).

INTRODUCTION

The literature abounds with works dealing with spy gadgetry and covert surveillance techniques; however, one must look far-and-wide to find details about constructing intelligence systems.[2] As we will see, a system for the storage and retrieval of information is at the center of any intelligence operation, yet there is somewhat less written about this aspect of intelligence.[3]

Despite the mystique surrounding such systems (i.e., as portrayed in television and cinema), it is conceptually a simple task to construct. You may even find that you are already practising, to some degree, the principles of sound information storage and retrieval.

The theory of intelligence systems is easy to grasp and straightforward to apply. We begin with a discussion about "What is Intelligence?" In this chapter, we visit the definition of *intelligence* and consider its advantages. We then look at the typology of intelligence, then its taxonomy, and finally, the intelligence process. These issues set the scene for our look at databases.

WHAT IS INTELLIGENCE?

The first step in understanding intelligence systems is to understand what is meant by *intelligence*. Intelligence has several meanings. First, it refers to knowledge, and secondly, it refers to the process in which knowledge is produced. It also refers to agencies or units within organizations that deal with knowledge. And finally, it refers to the reports and briefings produced in the process or by such bureaus.

---

2. For example, one rare source is, Jack Morris, *Police Intelligence Files: An Introduction to the Use of Confidential Police Files* (Orangevale, CA: Palmer Enterprises, 1983).

3. Sometimes referred to as *knowledge management systems* (abbreviated KMS); John McGonagle and Carolyn Vella, *Proactive Intelligence* (London: Springer, 2012), pp. 17–19.

As succinct as this definition is, some practitioners and academics continue to promote the idea that there is not an agreed definition. This, of course, is nonsense. As pointed out in *Methods of Inquiry for Intelligence Analysis, Third Edition*, "Although there may be as many definitions as intelligence scholars, the differences amount to mere wordsmithing. This is because the various definitions in circulation have commonalities that be narrowed to four meanings. Dictionaries use what is referred to as an 'order of definitions' in cases where there are multiple definitions."[4]

INFORMATION VERSUS INTELLIGENCE

Information is the raw material used to produce finished, focused intelligence. Without information, intelligence could not exist.

It is quite safe to say that every facet of our lives, whether central or incidental, is in some way related to information. We rely on an alarm clock to wake us in the morning (i.e., an information machine), news reports to tell us what is happening in the world beyond our doorstep, the smartphone app to tell us if will rain, an array of indicator lights and meters to tell us about our car's performance as we drive to work, traffic lights and signs to alert us to road conditions, and so on until our clocks yet again inform us that it is time to retire from the day's toil.

Individuals, organizations, and indeed whole societies survive on information. Civil society is only possible because of our ability to collect, store, retrieve, and transfer information from one person to another. The more complex our society, the more necessary it is to facilitate and support information management.[5]

---

4. Hank Prunckun, *Methods of Inquiry for Intelligence Analysis, Third Edition* (Lanham, MD: Rowman & Littlefield, 2019), p. 4.

5. Donald Cleveland and Ana Cleveland, *Introduction to Indexing and Abstracting* (Littleton, CO: Libraries Unlimited, 1983), p.18.

INTELLIGENCE AS KNOWLEDGE

Why should we be concerned with intelligence? "The answer is simple—because intelligence enables individuals and organizations who seek to exercise control over particular situations. In this sense, control equates to power."[6] Cohen in his classic treatment of the study of power writes:

> Power is sought because without power the security and even the ability of a state to continue to exist is generally decreased. Without power, a state has no ability to deter another . . . from actions whose consequences threaten the vital interests of the former. Without power, a state cannot cause another . . . to do that which the former desires but which the latter desires not to do. Power is sought because the more power that a state has, the greater is the number of its available options. The more options available to a state, the greater its security. The greater a state's security, the better off its people are. They are more secure in their life and in the enjoyment of their private property.[7]

To clarify, it is worth looking at examples in which the term *intelligence* is used. Intelligence as knowledge can be seen in the following hypothetical cases.

Law Enforcement Context

We have intelligence that indicates that Lucien DeJay is planning to break into the Pine Point branch office of Springfield Institution for Savings this Friday night.

---

6. Henry W. Prunckun, "First Principles of Intelligence Analysis: Theorizing a Model for Secret Research," in *Salus Journal*, Issue 3, Number 1, 2015, p. 31.

7. Ira S. Cohen, *Realpolitik: Theory and Practice* (Encino, CA: Dickenson Publishing, 1975), pp. 41–42.

Business Context

Intelligence suggests that Slezak Associates is about to begin an advertising campaign in the US northeast this autumn with the aim of capturing customers in the 25–45-year-old range.

Military Context

We have just received intelligence that supports earlier indications that the North Korean regime has authorized another nuclear weapons test. It will take place at their main site during the week celebrating the Supreme Leader's birth.

National Security Context

We have just received intelligence from Cuba that alerts us to the eminent passage of legislation legalising a multi-party, democratic political system.

TAXONOMY OF INTELLIGENCE

Intelligence has been classified into four taxonomical categories: basic, tactical, operational, and strategic.[8]

Basic Intelligence

- Provides an encyclopedia-like compilation of facts and figures relating to intelligence targets or possible targets;
- Covers a variety of topics, issues, events, situations, places, and people spanning many decades or even centuries;
- Can be used by research analysts as well as operational personnel; and
- Can be easily accessed for quick reference.

Tactical Intelligence

- Provides immediate information support an operation that is underway;
- Orientated toward an individual target or an activity over

---

8. Hank Prunckun, *Methods of Inquiry for Intelligence Analysis, Third Edition*, pp. 15–18.

the short term; and specific activities, or targets; and

- Provides day-to-day updates on unfolding events or developing situations.

Operational Intelligence

- Is short-range or time limited but usually covers a slightly longer time frame than tactical intelligence; and
- Consists of pattern, or operational mode activities that provide a wider perspective than does tactical intelligence.

Strategic Intelligence

- Provides a comprehensive picture of a target or activity;
- Comments on future prospects and the identification of potential problems;
- Generally considered a higher form of intelligence;
- Provides advice on capabilities, vulnerabilities, and intentions;
- Allows for adequate planning and policy development;
- Assists in resource allocation; and
- Requires extensive knowledge of specific targets and areas of activity.

INTELLIGENCE AS A PROCESS

The intelligence cycle is a process based on five steps or elements (see figure 1). This cycle is referred to as EEIs—essential elements of information.[9] At the start of the cycle, an information plan is formulated based on the research question, and those data are collected. The information is then collated (which is done when it is entered into the intelligence database), analyzed, and disseminated. These five steps are responsible for converting raw data into

---

9. U.S. Department of Defense, *Dictionary of Military and Associated Terms* (Washington, DC: USDoD, 2007), p. 75.

finished, focused intelligence.[10] The resulting intelligence is then considered by "consumers," thus completing, or restarting, the cycle depending on whether the question was answered, or new questions raised.

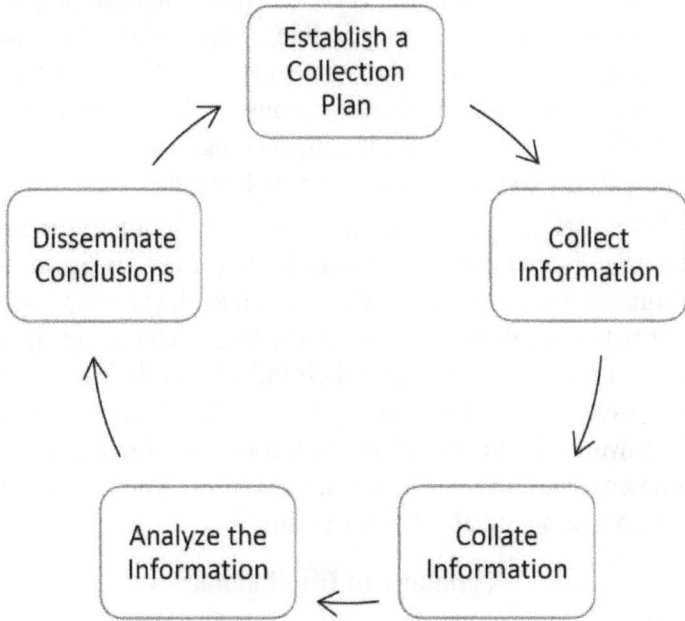

Figure 1—A simple version of the intelligence cycle.

INFORMATION COLLECTION

Information is collected from a variety of sources. Some examples of this diversity are listed below by category.[11] We

---

10. In more detail, the US Department of Defense says, "... [1] planning and direction, [2] collection, [3] processing and exploitation, [4] analysis and production, [5] dissemination and integration, and [6] evaluation and feedback," are the steps. USDoD, *Dictionary of Military and Associated Terms*, p. 108.

11. Although somewhat dated, Harry J. Murphy's reference work, *Where's What: Sources of Information for Federal Investigators* (New York: Quadrangle, 1975) provides many source ideas.

note that many of the sources of information are the same for like targets in the six different types of intelligence—national security, military, law enforcement, business, private, and humanitarian intelligence. [12]

It should be noted that it is conceivable that a single piece of information has a possible application to each typographical intelligence category. For example, information relating to a terrorist group could be of interest to domestic law enforcement intelligence agencies that have a responsibility to prevent and deter such attacks.

Likewise, the same information could be of interest to foreign policy and military intelligence if the terrorist group is internationally based. On the other hand, that same information might be of interest to business intelligence if the target of the terrorist group is their industry or their facilities. Similarly, private intelligence groups such as the anti-nuclear lobby would be interested in the information highlights, for argument sake, the vulnerable nature of nuclear facilities in relation to a potential act of terrorism.

Typology of Intelligence

Intelligence is structured according to type (or class), and the typology is based on the environment in which the organization operates. There are six types of intelligence: 1) national security (which includes foreign policy and international politics); 2) military; 3) law enforcement; 4) business; 5) private; and 6) humanitarian.[13] Some examples

---

12. Troy Whitford and Henry Prunckun, "Discreet, Not Covert: Reflections on Teaching Intelligence Analysis in a Non-Government Setting," in *Salus Journal*, vol. 5, no. 1, 2017, pp. 48–61.

13. Hank Prunckun, *Methods of Inquiry for Intelligence Analysis, Third Edition*, p. 26.

of the different sources of information of interest to each type is presented below.[14]

National Security Intelligence

- Open source information;
- Covert agents;
- Diplomatic missions and embassies;
- Surveillance satellites, aircraft and drones;
- Electronic intercepts;
- Defectors;
- University and independent research bodies; and
- Other government departments.

Military Intelligence

- Open source information;
- Surveillance planes;
- Surveillance satellites;
- Electronic intercepts;
- Covert agents;
- Diplomatic missions and embassies;
- Defectors;
- Prisoners;
- University and independent research bodies; and
- Other government departments.

Law Enforcement Intelligence

- The public;
- Investigators;
- Patrol Officers;
- Police records;
- The media;
- Business records;
- Government departments and agencies;

---

14. Patrick F. Walsh, *Intelligence, Biosecurity and Bioterrorism* (London: Palgrave Macmillan, 2018), pp. 89–92.

- Informants;
- Covert surveillance (physical, optical, and electronic);
- Undercover operatives; and
- Other law enforcement agencies and government departments.

Business Intelligence

- A business own internal records;
- Information supplied by other businesses;
- The media, trade and other open source publications;
- Sales personnel and customers;
- Distributors;
- Raw material and component suppliers;
- Government departments and agencies;
- A business research and development section(s);
- University and independent research bodies;
- Market research surveys;
- Reverse engineering; and
- Mystery shopping and similar methods of surveillance.

Private Intelligence[15]

- An organization's own internal records;
- Information supplied by other organizations;
- The media, trade and other open source publications;
- Staff;
- The public;
- Government departments and agencies;
- An organizations research section;
- University and independent research bodies;
- Surveys; and
- Covert physical surveillance.

---

15. See, Hank Prunckun, *Intelligence and Private Investigation: Developing Sophisticated Methods for Conducting Inquiries* (Springfield, IL: Charles C. Thomas, Ltd, 2013).

Humanitarian Intelligence

Because this type of intelligence is practiced by agencies engaged in humanitarian relief operations,[16] the sources of information are likely to include the other types of intelligence, though information supplied by national security, military, and law enforcement agencies are likely to be "sanitized" before being supplied (if at all) to humanitarian organizations.

EVALUATION OF INFORMATION

Decades ago, the International Association of Chiefs of Police recommended a set of guidelines relating to secret intelligence that are as relevant today as they were when they were made. The IACP said that "Law enforcement agencies constantly receive information from a variety of sources. All information must be evaluated to determine its relevance, completeness, and accuracy. ... When associations are not criminal in nature, or criminally related, the data should never be committed to file [i.e., folders]."[17]

As information is received it is evaluated according to:

- the reliability of the source (see table 1); and
- the validity of the actual information (see table 2).

When evaluating documents prior to collation, the following questions should be considered:

- How reliable is the information source?
- Has the source provided information before?
- How accurate is the information?
- How recent is the information?

---

16. Andrej Zwitter, *Humanitarian Intelligence: A Practitioner's Guide to Crisis Analysis and Project Design* (Lanham, MD: Rowman & Littlefield, 2016.

17. International Association of Chiefs of Police, *Law Enforcement Policy on the Management of Criminal Intelligence* (Gaitherburg, MD: IACP, 1985), pp. 8–9.

INFORMATION COLLATION

Collation is an intellectual process in which disparate pieces of information are brought together for the purpose of analysis. Information is collated to remove irrelevant, incorrect, or worthless information.[18]

The remaining (relevant) information is stored in a way that makes for effective and easy retrieval by researchers. This can be done by:

- Registering[19] the information in the storage system;
- Indexing the data;
- Cross-Referencing each data item; and
- Assigning keywords.

The information is then filed, and finally, the desired data is retrieved. Information is stored in a variety of forms:

- On corporate server databases;
- On workstation databases;
- In a word processing document(s);
- In hardcopy files; and
- In one's head as ideas and concepts.

---

18. The collection of irrelevant information will always occur through a multitude of reasons—errors of inadvertent inclusion, misdirection in the research question, or compulsiveness by analysts to collect "everything" in case it might, one day, be useful. Useless data should be destroyed as soon as it is identified. See the section on "Quality Control" for a discussion on purging unhelpful data.

19. *Registering* information is a formal logging process where a document (of any description) or a forensic artefact is recorded as being acquired from an external source or written/created/generated by an employee or officer of the agency.

Table 1—Source reliability codes.[20]

Admiralty Ratings		
Code	Descriptors	Estimated Truth Based on Past Reporting
A	Completely Reliable	100%
B	Usually Reliable	80%
C	Fairly Reliable	60%
D	Not Usually Reliable	40%
E	Unreliable	20%
F	Cannot be Judged	50%
G	Unintentionally Misleading	0%
H	Deliberately Deception	0%

Table 2—Information accuracy estimates.

Admiralty Ratings		
Code	Descriptors	Estimated Probability of Truth
1	Confirmed	100%
2	Probably True	80%
3	Possibility True	60%
4	Doubtful	40%
5	Improbable	20%
6	Cannot be Judged	50%
7	Misinformation	0%
8	Disinformation	0%

20. Tables 1 and 2 are from Hank Prunckun, *Methods of Inquiry for Intelligence Analysis, Third Edition*, pp. 44–45.

ANALYSIS OF INFORMATION

Information is analyzed, and inferences are developed about the activity, the person(s), the group(s) or organization(s) involved in the matter under investigation. In the most general terms, the steps in analyzing information are as follows:

- Examine the data;
- Sort facts from opinions;
- Combine with other information;
- Use an analytic method that is appropriate for the data;
- Develop inferences based on the findings;
- Draw conclusions that are within the limits of the data and the method used to analyze the information; and
- Make recommendations.

An analysis is based on sound quantitative and qualitative research methods.[21] This sometimes referred to as using "structured analytical techniques."[22]

DISSEMINATION OF INTELLIGENCE

Intelligence must be put into some sort of report[23] and disseminated to the appropriate users, known as *consumers*.[24] This may be in the form of:

---

21. Hank Prunckun, *Methods of Inquiry for Intelligence Analysis, Third Edition*, pp. 87–138.

22. Richards J. Heuer Jr. and Randolph H. Pherson, *Structured Analytic Techniques for Intelligence Analysis* (Washington, DC: CQ Press, 2011).

23. Charles C. Frost and Jack Morris, *Police Intelligence Reports: A Compendium on Police Intelligence Reporting Formats and Procedures* (Orangevale, CA: Palmer Enterprises, 1983).

24. David Mackay and Jerry H. Ratcliffe, "Intelligence Products and their Dissemination," in Jerry H. Ratcliffe, editor, *Strategic Thinking in Criminal Intelligence* (Sydney: The Federation Press, 2004), pp. 148–162.

- Reports;
- Memos;
- Minutes;
- Verbal briefings;
- Visual presentations; and
- Publications, though some may be classified.[25]

25. An example of classified publications is H. Bradford Westerfield, editor, *Inside CIA's Private World: Declassified Articles from the Agency's Internal Journal*, 1995–1992 (New Haven, CT: Yale University Press, 1995).

CHAPTER TWO
INTELLIGENCE SYSTEMS

DATA STORAGE AND RETRIEVAL

Information is stored for the purpose of retrieval. Information is not stored for the purpose of warehousing documents; it is worth repeating—it is stored to be retrieved. This may seem obvious, but in practice, this is not always the case.

Information retrieval is the selective yet systematic recall of stored information. To do this, the information must be stored logically. Otherwise, it may become lost "in the system."

Storing and retrieving data does not necessarily involve or require technology, but certainly, it helps. In most cases, it is unrealistic not to have it.

At the center of any intelligence system is some form of an index.[26] The purpose of the index is to facilitate the retrieval process. However, by creating an index to assist in the retrieval of information, by its nature, the index also imposes limits on how information can be retrieved. To compensate for this, a superior indexing system must be built. Such a system will allow for subjective, intuitive searching that is so much a part of good intelligence research. The types of indexes that we will consider are:

- Author indexes—people, organizations, corporate authors, government departments and agencies, universities, research foundations, and the like.
- Alphabetical Subject Indexes—headings, subheadings, cross-references, and qualifying terms.
- Keywords in Context—is a system specific to computerized systems. It operates by selecting

---

26. M. Harry, *The Muckraker's Manual: Handbook for Investigative Reporters* (Port Townsend, WA: Loompanics Unlimited, 1984), p. 97.

keywords appearing in the body of the text (for example, the keyword *blackmail* in a corruption report).

- Hierarchical Indexes—data items are arranged in a hierarchy, starting with topics of general scope, and progressing to more specific topics.
- Permuted Title Indexes—systematically rotating the words in the title of a document/folder.[27]

These types of indices are referred to as *metadata*. Metadata is data that supplies information about other data items. There are five categories of metadata, and they comprise: 1) descriptive metadata; 2) structural metadata; 3) administrative metadata; 4) reference metadata; and 5) statistical metadata.

For intelligence databases, we are interested in descriptive metadata—author, title, abstract, and keywords. These data are used to search for and identify documents that can help analysts answer their research questions.

Figure 2—A manual form of metadata.

---

27. The success of the permuted index depends on the accuracy of the person (original author, or where no title is given, as in the case of *ad hoc* papers, memos etc., the collector, writer, or researcher) creating the title to reflect the document/files content. This may be very difficult in the cases where a document/file covers several topics.

PRELIMINARY DATA ANALYSIS
Quality Control

To assist the analyst to determine the relevance of any particular piece of information to his/her project, a method of labelling each data item for its validity and hence the weight of credibility it is afforded in the final assessment is needed. This process was discussed previously in the section "Intelligence as a Process," under the subheading "Evaluation of Information."

If analysts can correlate their data with other sources of information considered reliable, then they theoretically increase the chances that the data is correct. Some intelligence agencies require that to take place before a data item is given an "A1" rating (see tables 1 and 2)—i.e., independently verified against two or more sources. However, as sensible as this seems, the process can be subject to phantom or ghost data that turn out to be self-validating.

By way of example, on a secret operation that the author was a member, the analytic team obtained a document that cited the occurrence of a particular meeting involving one of the operation's principal targets. If true, the information would have led to a significant breakthrough by piecing together a hitherto incomplete picture of the illegal industry that was under examination. So, the team set about checking the information with other sources, and sure enough, they came up with two independent confirmations! But something seemed odd. A couple of words in the information reports of the two additional sources were similar. As a result, the sources were checked against the two independent reports, and to the team's surprise, all three reports were based on a single report that was authored by yet another source!

As we see in this case, the data was self-validating. It does not need to be spelled out what the consequences would have been if an assessment was prepared on this data.[28] Prudent

---

28. But given the guidelines, it would have been correct.

advice is that an information validation system, such as the Admiralty rating (i.e., tables 1 and 2), should be only guidelines, not rules.

Periodic checks of an intelligence database should be carried-out to ensure that its integrity. One way to do this is by reconciling "look-a-like" headings and typographical errors. Obviously, we do not want or need two similar headings, and we will want to correct typos in names and so on.

By using a *report* option[29] in the database menu system, we can check for near matches in headings; for example, "book" and "books," or "Brown" and "Browne." Through such a report function, we can scroll through the print-to-screen report to identify headings that can be combined, thus eliminating a fragmented database.

Purging Information

Another aspect of quality control is purging redundant folders. Intelligence documents can accumulate quickly, and in turn, the folders that hold them, fill with material that is not always central to the project under study.

This is mostly due to the analyst's inability to predict what data they will need in the future, and hence, if a piece of information could be used, analysts tend to retain it.[30] However, at some stage, an assessment of information holdings should be done. Ideally, this should happen at the end of each research project or secret operation.

---

29. Commercial databases as well as custom programs have reporting options. From the application's report menu we can choose to print-to-screen, hardcopy, or print our search results to an electronic file (usually in several different formats; e.g., PDF, Rich text, plain text, Word, etc.).

30. Unless it is a fact that might be retained as part of the unit's basic intelligence holdings (see section "Basic Intelligence," under the subheading of Taxonomy of Intelligence, Chapter 1).

Information discovered to be irrelevant should be disposed of, and if found to have been inadvertently entered into the database, it should be purged. "The systematic purging of files [i.e., folders] according to fixed guidelines, ensures that data collected are criminally related and necessary to unit goals."[31]

During such an audit,[32] material that lacks accuracy, relevance, timeliness, or completeness, should be purged from the system. Retaining this material does nothing to improve the quality of an intelligence database, and if it is used in an intelligence assessment, the data will only detract from and possibly harm the report's conclusions.

Criteria for Retaining/Purging Information

Defensible—How reliable is the source? Are the conclusions that are drawn within the limits of the data and the analytic methods used?

Relevant—Does it supply the intelligence unit with information necessary to complete its project?

Timely—Does the information relate to the current project or operation?

Complete—Externally Obtained: Is the document source fully stated? Internally Generated: Are the facts referred to in the report, chart, assessment, etc., footnoted or otherwise refer the reader to the source[33]/authority? General: Are comments and inferences by analysts clearly indicated and distinct from verified facts?

---

31. IACP, *Law Enforcement Policy on the Management of Criminal Intelligence*, p. 9.

32. Jack Morris, Michael McMullen, Gregory Stock, Dick Wright, and Gary Petersen, *Criminal Intelligence Programs for the Smaller Agency* (Sacramento, CA: California Peace Officers' Association, 1988), pp. 24 and 27.

33. Except the identity deep cover/covert sources, and other human and technical vulnerable sources.

When information lacking these qualities is discovered, it should be subject to upgrading in the first instance. But, if the cost of validating or verifying this information proves to be more than the potential value of the resulting data, the data should then be removed.

This process should, preferably, be done on a project-by-project, operation-by-operation basis.[34]   In this way, validating and verifying can be done with ease and effectiveness while the project is still fresh in the minds of the researchers. Likewise, the accuracy of an index should be maintained daily—corrections and updates should be done as they are encountered. This makes for both efficient and effective management of time and of the database.

A bi-yearly quality control exercise should be done on the whole database. The criteria just discussed can be applied to the data and upgraded and/or discarded when encountered. In some intelligence agencies, if data cannot be judged, the document is sent to the originator of the report or provider of the information (e.g., a field operative) and asked to upgrade it or otherwise provide clarifying comments. The upgraded data is then entered into the system, *replacing* the old. If it cannot be upgraded, the data should be removed.

Soundex Searches

Soundex is an indexing method that encodes data items for retrieval. Soundex searching is a way of looking for an information item where the exact spelling is unknown, misspelled, or, as in the case of names, difficult to pronounce.[35]

Because the Soundex searching relies on phonetic spelling, a search is likely to be more reliable if carried out for single words rather than combinations, such as titles and

---

34.   M. Harry, *The Muckraker's Manual: Handbook for Investigative Reporters*, pp. 98 and 101.

35.   Originally developed by Margaret K. Odell and Robert C. Russell [cf. U.S. Patents 1261167(1918), 1435663(1922)].

phrases. Therefore, when indexing only a single words are used and that this word is a significant name from the document's heading or subheading field. The name can be a business name, an unusual trade or brand name, or an acronym.[36]

---

36. The Soundex method of indexing involves four steps; "...1) Retain the first letter of the name, and drop all occurrences of a, e, h, i, o, u, w, y, in other positions. 2) Assign the following numbers to the remaining letters after the first: 1 = b, f, p, v; 2 = c, g, j, k, q, s, x, z; 3 = d, t; 4 = l; 5 = m, n; 6 = r. 3) If two or more letters with the same code were adjacent in the original name (before step 1), omit all but the first. 4) Convert to the form 'letter, digit, digit, digit' by adding trailing zeros (if there are more than three)." Donald E. Knuth, *The Art of Computer Programming*, Volume 3/ Sorting and Searching, (Reading, MA: Addison-Wesley Publishing Company, Inc., 1973), pp. 391–392.

CHAPTER THREE
CREATING AN INTELLIGENCE SYSTEM

INTRODUCTION

Information is useless unless it can be located and retrieved. What we will now discuss, is a *model intelligence system* that can be scaled up and adapted for a variety of applications—a specific project, a series of like projects, or target profiles, tactical assessments, or factual dossiers about persons-of-interest.

There is an adage that says, "information is power." However, it could be argued that this is not entirely true, because information in its raw form is no more powerful than the wave created when a stone is thrown into an ocean.

Information becomes power only after it is collated, analysed, interpreted, and then applied to answer a specific question. Power from information comes only when it is blended with other facts to derive meaning. The ability to derive meaning from raw information is how power is developed.[37]

Likewise, no matter how good a team of analysts is, and no matter how vast their information holdings are, if they cannot identify and retrieve a particular piece of information from the system when they need it,[38] it becomes clear that information is *not* power.

To build a professional intelligence system, it must be simple (otherwise no one will use it), easy to understand (again, no one will use it), and it must work. This may sound like common sense, but the author has seen intelligence

---

37. Sun Tzu, *The Art of War*, 1983).

38. Or are flooded with search results, drowning the vital data item in the tsunami of findings.

systems that do not meet these modest standards, and researchers struggle to make them run.

Moreover, a system must be able to store an item and allow an analyst to retrieve it, say, three years hence without going through the scenario of, "...was it indexed under 'Hong Kong, independence movement,' 'pro-democracy activists,' or 'Chinese Communist Party, critics'," or some other descriptor that has since slipped from their memory, or vanished when the researcher who had knowledge of the matter left to take-up employment in another agency.

Put another way, an intelligence database is not a group of binders holding disparate collections of old and fading newspaper clippings. Nor is it a series of filing cabinets stuffed to overflowing. And it is not a server rack holding terabytes of digital records. An intelligence database is a system that allows for the efficient integration, indexing, and cross-indexing of information that also offers some rudimentary level of collation (i.e., value added though a variety of report generation functions), ready for analysis and interpretation.

BACKGROUND

When creating an intelligence database, analysts have several different options. At one time in history, the most common was the manual filing system. This consisted of having a system of hardcopy folders created to hold all the material relating to a project or operation. Then, in the early-1980s, came affordable computerization.

From about the early-1990s onwards, a computerized intelligence system becomes the default choice.[39] Unless for some reason—such as a small task that is narrowly focused, or limited in duration—a manual filing system would unlikely take preference over a digital database.

---

39. Steven Gottlieb, Sheldon Arenberg, and Raj Singh, *Crime Analysis* (Montclair, CA: Alpha Publishing, 1994), pp. 131–132.

So, an intelligence system can consist of a manual indexing system or can extend to a fully integrated system consisting of 100% electronic data capture and search. The latter needs procedures and facilities to convert all data (for example, letters, reports, memos, photographs, diagrams, and so on) to electronic format by direct data conversion, usually through some forms of scanning or an audio transcription.

Once these data are converted, the system would provide for document indexing (at a paragraph-by-paragraph and page-by-page level, as well as whole-of-document level). Retrieval would also be automated, allowing researchers to view a range of documents directly on their monitor, and to copy-and-paste useful material (both text and imagery) to the report, they are writing. The intelligence report itself would be retained in the system, and it too would be indexed for future retrieval.

First, we will examine the classic manual system. Why? Because the theory that underpins a manual system is the same theory that supports digital databases. Arguably, the only difference is how each is structured.

A paper-based system may be constructed using folders containing several documents, as can a digital database. Whatever structure a manual system comprises, its electronic equivalent can also. In addition, a digital database can incorporate several search and retrieval mechanisms, whereas a manual system cannot.

In a small business intelligence project such as a background examination of a new company coming into the market, this may consist of perhaps between a ten and one hundred documents. An easy amount to fit into a single folder cover. However, if the project is a detailed police investigation into, say, and organized crime target, then there will no doubt be several dozen to several hundred folders created to deal with the amount of material collected.[40] Not only will the collected data be a formidable task to physically handle, but the synthesis of these data into reports, assessments, legal briefs, and so on, is likely to generate many additional documents and folders that also need processing.

As all this happens, it will be imperative that analysts are able to identify the original documents (primary data) from the distilled/analyzed (secondary, tertiary, quaternary, etc.) data. Otherwise, they will encounter problems where future assessments are based on the conclusions/interpretations of secondary information and not the primary data. This can lead to incorrect plans, actions, and recommendations.

MANUAL INTELLIGENCE SYSTEMS

The following discussion addresses the manual "index card" system. It is the traditional method for creating an intelligence system. The manual system has been used for centuries in a variety of fields. It is explored here, not because it is likely to rally a comeback over computerized systems, but because it explains the fundamentals of digital systems. After all, the principles of manual systems gave birth to what analysts use now.

Filing versus Indexing

Filing is the storing of documents (and other data artefacts such as photographs, and audio recordings) so that:

a.   they are protected from loss and physical damage; and,

b.   they can be retrieved easily.

Indexing on the other hand is the "key" to how the documents are stored in the filing system. What we are interested in here is a specific type of filing system—an intelligence database.

What you will be trying to achieve when you create such

---

40. One investigation into organized crime that the author worked on had seventeen thousand (yes, 17,000!) folders relating to the case.

a system is to avoid losing documents in the system, which can happen in any type of work that involves volumes of data. It happened so often in one intelligence agency in which the author worked, field operatives referred to the system as "the black hole."

Traditional Filing Systems

The traditional way intelligence agencies stored and retrieved information about targets or about the progress of secret operations was the simple filing system. This type of system consists of large numbers of individual folders, each containing data relating to a particular topic—for example, "arms dealing." These documents are given titles or subject headings that are indexed. They are then stored according to the agency's filing policy. For instance, they may have been stored in hardcopy horizontal filing cabinets or compactus for, say, several years; then they may be destroyed after their contents have been microfilmed. Now, these film records are being digitized (see figure 3).

Figure 3—Digital conversion of microfilm records.

When researchers used this type of system, they approached the index and looked up the appropriate title or subject heading, and if everything is working properly, the system returned the folders storage reference. Then it was a matter for walking to the storage room or device and extracting the folder(s).[41]

Continuous Document Filing

One way some researchers overcame the problem of creating files and indexing each paragraph, page, and document was to use the continuous filing system. The procedure for this system was to file each document as it was received and numbering it progressively.

This system required each page of a, for example, right-wing political brochure, to be treated as a separate document. In this way, information about each document could be linked to a notional electronic file.

The notional electronic folder, as its name suggests, did not exist in the real world, but was merely a collection of references (to documents) connected or linked to the file number via the structure of the database (this is the same whether it is manual or electronic).

Let us take a minute to see how this type of system worked.

1. A document is received from a field operative or other source;
2. It is given the next sequential number. For the purposes of this example, it will be notional number 00000241183.
3. It is evaluated for relevant information (see the previous section on "Collation of Information"). It is found that it contains details that were useful to the unit's project on pharmaceutical research.
4. It is given a suitable title ("Foreign hacking of pharmaceutical research projects…"), and keywords in point 3 above are then noted;

---

41. See Appendix A for ideas for small-scale manual filing equipment.

5. The data mentioned in point 4 above (title and keywords) is then entered into the database (either by an automated process as the document is scanned or manually entered) against the document number 00000241183; and

6. Finally, this index is linked to one or more secret projects or operations; for instance, "foreign interference," "industrial espionage," "trade secrets," etc.

If we examine the system, we see we have a filing system that consists of documents numbered from one to infinity, filed in several different ways (e.g., filing cabinets, compactus, rolls of microfilm, flat sheets of microfiche, and so on). We then have that document number linked to a variety of keywords, subjects, and a title, with those words/title linked to a project(s) and/or operation(s).

Therefore, when researchers want to see the material on a project regarding "foreign interference," they interrogate the system where it reports all documents linked to that search term. In an electronic system, analysts are presented with the documents on their monitors.

Indexing and Titling

The manual system is based on what was 3-inch by 5-inch index cards. Information was recorded by hand or typed and stored in a horizontal file box. Entries were arranged according to one of the indexing methods that we will now discuss.

Indexing Systems

There are basically six types of indexing systems, all of which can be adopted for intelligence purposes. These systems are the alphabetical system, the numeric system, the geographical system, the subject system, hierarchical system, and the permuted title system.

Alphabetical Systems. The alphabetical system, as its name indicates, relies on the alphabet to arrange documents. The best example of this is the telephone book. If we imagine that we are putting together dossiers on various businesses, organizations, and individuals, an alpha system, like the telephone book, would be the simplest and most effective way of filing our data. There is really no confusion—if we want to see what the holdings on "Lucian DeJay," we'd go to the Ds and look-up "D-E-J-A-Y." And from there we have it—Lucian's dossier.[42]

Now, if we want to also incorporate other material into the intelligence system, such as a company's annual report, we start to develop problems—take for instance an investigation into financial issues of, say, "Mossack Fonseca & Co." or do we index under "annual reports," or some other heading?

The problem can get even more complicated if, for example, we obtained the annual report not in relation to the Panamanian law firm *per se*, but in relation to Ramón Fonseca, one of the founders of the legal firm. So, do we file it under "Fonseca, Ramón" or "Mossack Fonseca & Co.?" What if we want it in both places, and for that matter, in more places, such as under "Panama" where its headquarters was located?

One answer, which is *not* recommended, is to make photocopies of all documents and place them on each

---

42. Documents within a dossier can be arranged from the most recent acquisition on top, descending to the oldest document on the bottom, or in other words, chronological order. For those documents that do not have clearly identifiable author, date, source markings, a rubber stamp such as that shown in Appendix B can be used. In this way, an analyst conducting future research can make a quick assessment of the relevance of the document to his/her project. Without it, such documents may become useless information.

entity's[43] file or dossier. The better way is to file the annual report by itself with multiple index cards pointing researchers to that document. Of course, in a digital system, this is how it would work—one digital copy with pointers to it.

Let us go back to our manual system to see how that would work. If we want to examine "Ramón Fonseca," we go to our index and look-up "Fonseca." We then see that there are several cards for that entry. The first says, "Fonseca—Portuguese winery"; the second says, "Fonseca, Ramón—cofounder of Mossack Fonseca & Co."; the third says, "Fonseca, Ramón—Germany issued international arrest warrants for him and his firm's other cofounder, Jürgen Mossack"; the fourth says, "Fonseca—novelist, lawyer and politician"; and the fifth and last entry says, "Fonseca—in relation to the publication of the 'Panama Papers'."

So, we can select the index card with reference to Fonseca's role as founder of the law firm and go directly to that document(s). Likewise, if we were interested in Fonseca's controversial role in the "Panama Papers" we would look under "Fonseca—in relation to the publication of the 'Panama Papers'." The index reference would indicate the same document(s); there is no need to photocopy the document(s) multiple times and create numerous files.

This is an efficient way to handle data in a small-scale project, or where the original document(s) was retained for evidentiary proposes. It is also the way documents are managed in an electronic database; that is, a single digitized document is retained of the system, but through the user interface (e.g., menus), researchers are able to retrieve them without the worry findings its physical location.

Numeric Systems. An improvement to the alphabetical system is the numeric system because it allows for easy

---

43. An entity can be a person, telephone number, an establishment, a vehicle, an address, an aircraft, other forms of numbers, a ship/boat, a travel movement, and goods/services.

expansion. Unlike the alphabetic system that requires re-shelfing of folders (sometimes, in large numbers) to make room for new folders that are added (for example, when the shelf containing "A" folders becomes full, you will have to move some of the "B" folders over so that more "A" folders can be added), expansion is uninhibited under the numeric system.

In this system, each new document is given a number from a continuous, sequential number allocation. As new documents are added to the agency's holdings, they can be filed at the end of the shelf next to the last number.

Although the numeric system is less trouble to maintain in terms of shelf reorganisation, it has disadvantages when retrieving documents pertaining to a target. Analysts may have thirty folders containing information relating to the subject under study, and it is more than likely that these folders will be spread throughout the filing system because they would have been added to the holdings at different times during the collection phase. Furthermore, retrieval of these documents relies upon an alphabetical index to identify the document number to be retrieved.

But not so if this method is computerized. The document, photograph, or other pieces of information are stored in the system, and an e-pointer is made to a folder (or folders), and like the hardcopy method, index references are assigned. In this way, when researchers search for, say, Fonseca, they are presented with a list of relevant folders. And, by selecting one-or-other folders displayed on their monitor, they can see the documents that comprise the folder. Of course, some documents may appear in multiple folders, but it will be the same e-copy stored on the server.

Geographical Systems. The geographical system is another system for storing data. This system calls for data to be filed alphabetically by geographical location rather than by name.

This is a useful system for some types of businesses or government agencies (for example, sporting bodies, religious organizations, and professional societies). It is not specific enough to be relied upon *solely* by intelligence researchers; nevertheless, its features can be incorporated into an intelligence system.

As an example, let us imagine that analysts have a system that has numerous alphabetical headings As such, they could add geographical headings on a sub-index level, pointing researchers to documents if the topic/subject can be described by a geographical location. For instance, "Panama—alleged money laundering by Mossack Fonseca & Co."

Subject Filing. A subject index is another system that has application for intelligence databases. The subjects are arranged in alphabetical order according to terms standardized by the system's thesaurus.[44] The subject matter system by itself is likely to be too broad to be the main method of indexing intelligence information, especially for a manual system. This is analogous to the Dewey Decimal Classification method used by libraries to index books (figure 4). Researchers would most likely need to refine this type of index to assist searching.

Having said that, if a subject filing system was computerized, it could be structured as the main heading, with any number of other methods as subheadings—such as, "Panama" as the first-level heading, followed by names, entities, dates, or other types of subheadings.

Rotational Filing System. Rotational (title) indices[45] systematically rotate the words in the title of a document/folder. The success of the rotational index depends upon the accuracy of the person (original collector/author or where no title is given, as in the case of *ad hoc* papers, memos etc., the collector, writer, or researcher) creating the title to

---

44. See the section "Thesaurus" in Chapter 4.
45. Sometimes referred to as a mutation index (or permuted index) because the system requires analysts to mutate (i.e., rotate) the words in the title to facilitate retrieval.

reflect the document's/folder's content. This may be difficult in cases where a document/folder covers several topics.

An example of a rotational (title) heading might appear like a book title—Jürgen Mossack: Cofounder of the legal firm Mossack Fonseca & Co. and his role in the "Panama Papers" scandal.

Figure 4—Books filed according to the
Dewey Decimal System.

The Ultimate System. The definitive intelligence system incorporates all the aforementioned features—alphabetical, numeric, geographical, subject-matter, and rotational (title) indexes—in one system. A good intelligence database will allow researchers to search for a target or subject in several different ways—"Fonseca, Ramón"; "Panama—money laundering"; "Panama Papers—release of by the International Consortium of Investigative Journalists," "Data Leak—brother-in-law of China's General Secretary Xi Jinping" who was named in leaked Panama Papers,[46] and the like.

---

46. "Panama Papers: The Power Players," International
–continued–

All methods will locate documents relating to this firm's alleged activities regarding money laundering and tax evasion. These references will prompt researchers to make other inquiries of the system until they are satisfied with the depth of data retrieved and can begin their analysis.

If there is not enough information in the agency's holdings, analysts can then outline what types of data they need to answer their research question ("What business venture is likely to attract Jürgen Mossack now?).[47]

COMPUTERIZED INTELLIGENCE SYSTEMS

Until August 1981, when IBM introduced its "PC" model microcomputer, only agencies with sizeable budgets could afford computerized intelligence databases. With the advent of massed produced computers a few years later, the ability to store large amounts of information came within reach of everyone. And, as we saw in the previous section on manual intelligence systems, a single document can require many, many index cards.

If researchers expect their projects to go for some time (e.g., an environmental lobby group) or a project to be large (e.g., crime/corruption data), then a manual system may be unrealistic. Computerized systems are the only answer to a credible intelligence system. Though, having said that, there is likely to always be a manual filing system for some intelligence material—take, for instance, material that might one day be needed for forensics analysis.

A computerized filing system is based on the manual system. It is essentially the same; however, there are advantages of having intelligence information recorded

---

Consortium of Investigative Journalists. https://www.icij.org/investigations/panama-papers/the-power-players/, accessed 9 November 2020.

47. Refer to the section on "The Intelligence Process" for a discussion on the intelligence cycle.

digitally. Apart from the obvious fast retrieval of a particular information item, there are other benefits:

- Retrieve information according to a variety of search parameters;
- Create new databases from the original database;
- Optimize data integrity by ensuring stringent quality control measures (error checking, duplication, etc.);
- Provide statistical information needed to assess effectiveness;
- Menu drive for confusion-reduced searching;
- Multiple users (i.e., in a network situation); and
- A variety of search reports.

Computerized Intelligence Concepts

The central concepts of computerized intelligence databases are *data* (or, *information*), *file*, *record*, and *template*.

Data. The term *data* refers to individual pieces of information about a subject or target. For example, a person's name, address, telephone number, date of birth, and so on. There are three types of data: numeric data, textual data, and pictorial data. Numeric data can be calculated, whereas textual and pictorial cannot.[48]

"Some intelligence scholars make a distinction between the terms *data* and *information*. … Trying to create a distinction between these two terms, in contrast to common usage, could be said to be an exercise in abstractness that adds nothing to our understanding, but does add to our confusion."[49] So, from our perspective, *data* is *information*.[50]

---

48. Technically, there is also date data, and logical data (i.e., true/false, yes/no), but these are considered to be categorical data, and hence, can be analyzed statistically.

49. Hank Prunckun, *Methods of Inquiry for Intelligence Analysis, Third Edition*, p. 7.

50. Note that the term data is both singular and plural.

File. A computerized intelligence system enables analysts to set up files to store data under various headings. Files in this sense should not be confused with hardcopy files that we will refer to as *folders*.

Data contained in a file will differ from file-to-file, and the type of data it contains will also differ, as will the way it is organized or structured. One file may record name, address, telephone number, and customer account numbers. Another may contain a name, accounts outstanding, etc. (change these example to more intel type). So, a computer-created file is an organized body of data. It is commonly referred to as a *database*.

Record. A record is an individual unit held in an electronic file. An example of this is the information relating to one single entry. This consists of a heading, subheading, etc. Together these data items constitute a *record*.

Field. A field is a single data item. As mentioned previously, a record consists of one or more data items—heading, subheading, etc. Each item is termed a *field*. The structure of a record is determined by the number of fields it contains, the length of the fields, the type of fields (characters, dates only, or logical operators—true/false, yes/no).

Template. A template is the structure of the computer file or database without any data in it. Designing a database starts with laying out a template. In doing so, we need to determine the type of information we want to record (logic, date, character or numeric data), the size or amount of data (field length) and the fields identifying names (labels).

Commercial Database Applications

Once a template has been constructed, researchers need to decide how the data will be entered into the system, and later, how it can be retrieved. That is, what will the menu system (i.e., the system's "front end") look like? Will it incorporate other features to make the researchers' job easier (rather than entering in long, repetitive Boolean-type command each time retrieval is required).[51]

Although there are many database software packages on the market today, and new ones being released regularly, the better applications will be quick, easy to use and to have a clean, uncomplicated visual interface.

Relational versus Non-Relational Databases

Relational databases are programs that relate the information in two or more computer files to one another. They are used in making data storage as efficient as possible. In the example below, the PIN (personal identification number) is the field that "relates" the two database files. This type of database is useful where data is to be stored in many fields. In this way, the secondary (and tertiary, quadentary, and so on...) databases folders are only used and hence occupy space on the server's storage drive, when data is inserted, thus saving space (see figure 5).

On the other hand, non-relational databases (sometimes referred to as *card-box* databases) can only handle one file at a time. These types of databases lend themselves to situations that do not demand many fields; for example, where there is no dependence on multiple fields. In these cases, such a simple structure can efficiently store information in a non-relational configuration.

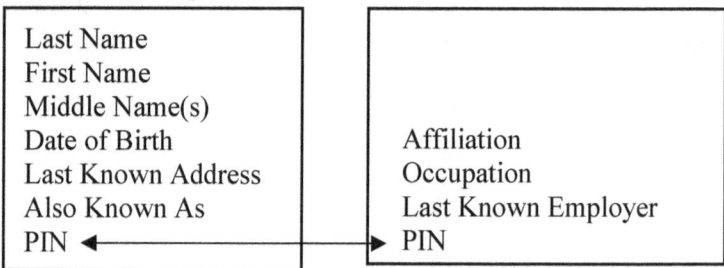

Last Name	
First Name	
Middle Name(s)	
Date of Birth	Affiliation
Last Known Address	Occupation
Also Known As	Last Known Employer
PIN ◄─────────────► PIN	

Figure 5—Logical model of a relational database.

---

51. Such features might include, adding and deleting records, updating records, validating data, searching for records, and producing reports.

CHAPTER FOUR
BUILDING A COMPUTERIZED INTELLIGENCE SYSTEM

IT'S A STEPWISE PROCESS

Step 1. Determine the scope of the system. What are the boundaries? Where will the system end and where will other systems begin? Will this system relate to other non-intelligence systems?[52]

Step 2. Determine what the system will do. Had the target user group been identified? Who will use the data, and what outputs will the system produce for them? Define the types of reports required, what information will these reports contain, what they will look like to the user, how often they need to be produced, and so on?

Step 3. Determine what data will need to be input. This will rely, to a large extent, on the output requirements of the intelligence projects being undertaken. But analysts should also consider ways to arrange the raw data to ease the strain on staff entering the information. This also helps reduce input errors (remember, bad data equals bad results). Also, include checks to validate data to reduce database corruption.

Step 4. Design the system. This step calls for a template to be created according to input/output needs and in accordance with researchers' determinations as to inputting ease (i.e., the order of data items). Second, design the reports that are to be produced. And lastly, set-up the front-end menu structure and functionality for reports and other database aspects.

Step 5. Test the system. Enter test data into the new database and check that everything works according to what was planned. For instance, are analysts getting the records they

---

52. See the section on "Relational versus Non-Relational Databases" the previous chapter.

requested? Are the reports in the format specified, and do they contain the correct (test) data items?

Step 6. Maintenance of the Database. When the database is complete, researchers will need to consider the problem of maintenance. Who will maintain the database—that is, not the technical maintenance (which is done by the IT department) but the maintenance of the information items? The integrity of the database's information will need to be checked regularly. Many intelligence units have "Information Managers," "Information Control Officers," or "Data Administrators," specifically for this purpose.

THESAURUS

The key to storage and retrieval is indexing, titling, and keywording. Because without these, the folder and its information may as well not exist—no one will be able to find what they need. This cannot be stressed too strongly. If there is a failure to put enough thought into the cataloging of intelligence data, analysts will find it difficult to discover documents or, worse, will not find the material at all.

A thesaurus is one way of standardizing the way folders are indexed, titled, and given keywords. A thesaurus identifies a word that encompasses a range of other words with similar meanings. For instance, a thesaurus for crime investigation may have "motorcycle gang" as a thesaurus entry. This entry is used whenever a reference is made to it or one of its synonyms, such as "biker gang," "bikers,"[53] etc.

By using the same word from the thesaurus, both the data collector and the registry clerk[54] can standardize the entry. With the use of a thesaurus, researchers can minimize the

---

53. These are terms used in the US, whereas "bikies" is used in Australian and New Zealand. So, it may also need to take international perspective if projects have a transnational dimension.

54. The role of a registry clerk is the process the agency's documents, facilitate access to, and security of, the database.

time it takes to retrieve the material they need. Confident that entries have been made consistent, analysts can examine any entries for "motorcycle gangs," rather than spending time hunting through entries for "biker gangs," "bikers," and so forth.

A thesaurus entry for every topic of inquiry can be made. To assist, many thesauruses exist that can be adopted wholly or used to tailor a unit's thesaurus (we need to be mindful not breach copyright). An exemplar of one such off-the-shelf thesauruses is the US National Criminal Justice Reference Service's thesaurus. Thesaurus term searches allow researchers to locate material in the NCJRS's *Abstracts Database* using its "controlled vocabulary." The NCJRS's controlled vocabulary helps assign indexing terms to the documents stored in its collection. At the time of this writing, the thesaurus was accessible online.

HOW TO CREATE A THESAURUS

A thesaurus is used in both manual and computerized intelligence systems. Creating one is a relatively simple task. After a document has been given a titled, analysts identify words that they consider key (hence the term *keyword*).

Once this has been done, researchers can start to make a keyword book or thesaurus. This guide will hold the list of keywords common to the type of intelligence work/research projects an agency is involved—national security, military, law enforcement, business, private, or humanitarian.

This compilation needs to be crafted with a reasonable degree of thought to make it work. However, remember that there is no right or wrong way to compose a keyword list. What may be key to one analyst's project may not be key to another researcher.

By way of example, a thesaurus for an intelligence database being developed by a law enforcement unit looking at allegations of corruption amongst public officials may include "bribery." Synonyms for this term may include those shown in figure 6.

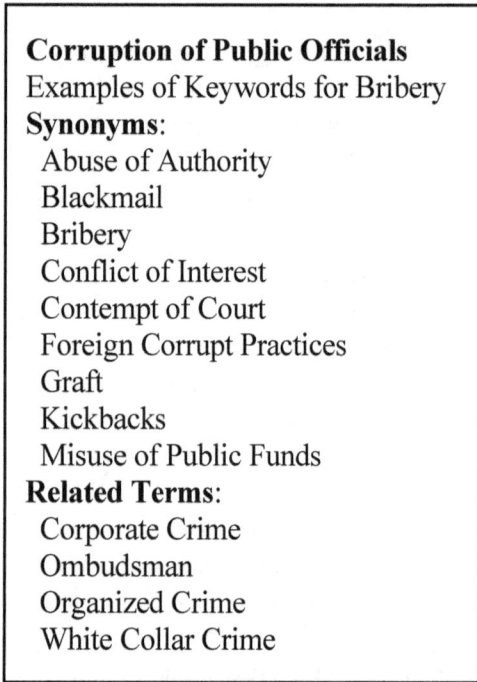

Corruption of Public Officials
Examples of Keywords for Bribery
Synonyms:
  Abuse of Authority
  Blackmail
  Bribery
  Conflict of Interest
  Contempt of Court
  Foreign Corrupt Practices
  Graft
  Kickbacks
  Misuse of Public Funds
Related Terms:
  Corporate Crime
  Ombudsman
  Organized Crime
  White Collar Crime

Figure 6—Examples of Synonyms

Within the thesaurus, pointers are placed at each synonym to guide the researcher to the keyword. For example, see figure 7.

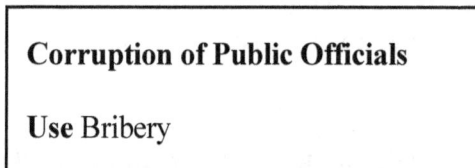

Corruption of Public Officials

Use Bribery

Figure 7—Synonym Pointers

There are two other terms used to qualify the synonyms in the thesaurus. *Use* terms are synonyms or near synonyms (figure 4). *Used for* terms (figure 8) are the opposite of *Use* terms. *Use for* shows the researcher that the descriptor is included in the keyword.

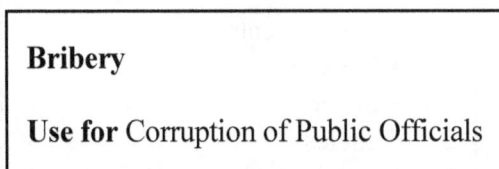

Bribery

Use for Corruption of Public Officials

Figure 8—"Use for" terms

Related terms (figure 9) are words or phrases that clarify the main term or alerts researchers to other terms.

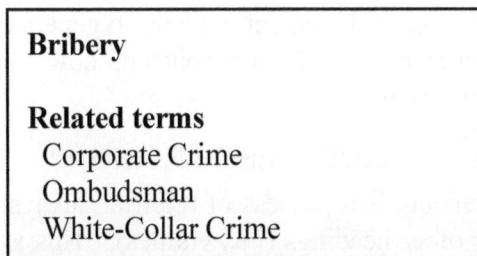

Bribery

Related terms
Corporate Crime
Ombudsman
White-Collar Crime

Figure 9—"Related terms"

ENTITIES

Every *key* entity in a document should be indexed as well as its associates if any (figure 10). For instance, in a company, we are looking for the chairperson (or presiding member), directors, company secretary, advisers, president, vice-presidents, treasurer, auditors, and anyone else who appears to be important to the company. Remember, *key* people—the photographer who took the glossy pictures for the glossy annual report may not be critical unless she is related/associated with any of the intelligence targets.

Entities

1   Persons
2   Establishments
3   Addresses
4   Numbers
5   Vehicles
6   Aircraft
7   Watercraft
8   Goods
9   Services

Figure 10—Examples of Entities

It is usual that each document is likely to generate up to ten or twelve index entries. It all depends on how "information rich" the document is.

CROSS-REFERENCING

Cross-referencing is a process of referring analysts to other data and/or other headings (i.e., entities). This is shown in figure 11. If we have an index entry for the heading "spying," our thesaurus will find that the heading we devise is, for argument sake, "espionage." The index card would read:

Spying

see Espionage
also see Data Collection; Information Gathering;
Surveillance; Intercepts

Figure 11—Example of Cross-Referencing

The *see* refers to the *use for* term from the thesaurus, and the *also see* refers to the *related terms* discussed. Cross-referencing can enhance the analyst's search by providing a reminder to think of other possible headings to make inquiries.[55]

DOCUMENT/FOLDER TRACKING

The sole purpose of storing data is to retrieve it. One of the most critical rules to establish and follow is that any folder or document removed from the system needs to be tracked. The borrower must be able to be identified should the paper folder be needed by another person. In an electronic system, this can be done by logging the retrieval (day, time, and length of time it was opened, as well as if copies were printed or the data downloaded[56]).

Folder tracking can be done in several ways, but a popular method is to have an index card inserted in a pocket of the folder that cites the folder's number. The borrower's name is then written on the card with the date borrowed and when it was returned, as is the case with library books. The next person to borrow the folder is then listed on the line below, and so on until the card is full.[57] Once this occurs, another

---

55. And when engulfed in a project, it is often difficult to remember to do everything all the time.

56. "Illustration this point is the alleged leaking in 2010 by Private First-Class Bradley Manning, and intelligence analyst with the US Army stationed in Iraq, of some 250,000 classified documents to the WikiLeaks organization." Hank Prunckun, *Counterintelligence Theory and Practice, Second Edition* (Lanham, MD: Rowman & Littlefield, 2019), p. 9.

57. In a manual filing system, when an analyst takes possession of a folder from the agency's holdings, an indicator card should be used to show the temporary removal of the folder from the system. This also helps refile the documents when they are returned.

index card is stapled to the first card and on the entries go.[58] This not only records who currently has what data, but it also facilitates an "audit trail." In other words, it shows who has accessed the information. This can be valuable in the case of where classified information has been leaked, and a counterintelligence investigation[59] is underway.

A FINAL WORD

Garbage In, Garbage Out

Technology and cleverly designed applications will not guarantee the integrity of the information they hold. Information collators and data entry staff must be motivated and exercise a great deal of discipline when handling intelligence. A high level of personal skill and ability is needed to identify, and sometimes intuitively select, entities for indexing. Therefore, a great deal of effort needs to be provided in the data input stage.

When mistakes are made, they need to be corrected; immediately. If care is exercised at the beginning, the hard work of extracting will be done by "the system" in the end— the way it should be. After all, doing the hard work is the system's job—retrieval. Computerized systems can and should be designed for ease of input, but this is not their central role *per se*. Data storage and retrieval is.

---

58. *Dead* index cards, on the other hand, should be removed from a manual filing system when dead documents/folders are removed. See the section that discusses culling intelligence documents.

59. Hank Prunckun, *Counterintelligence Theory and Practice, Second Edition*, 2019.

APPENDIX A
FILING EQUIPMENT EXPLAINED

Filing Cabinets

The most common filing equipment in use today is arguably the drawer filing cabinet. They are commercially available in two, three, and four drawer configurations.

Open-Shelf Files

Open-shelf files consist of multiple shelves in cabinets or cases that hold folders identified by name (alphabetical), number, or color codes inscribed on the side of the folder.

Rotary Files

Rotary files range from desk-top wheels of cards to large, motorized index or data revolving circular bins.

Horizontal Files

These are shallow tray type cabinets that normally hold large documents that require them to be laid flat—for example, photographs, maps, building plans, and so on.

Book or Binder Folders

These hold documents via a system of two or three holes punched along the left-hand side and held in place by a metal clasp, metal spring-ring, or simply by closed ring configuration. These type of folders are more in the category of temporary filing equipment and should not be considered for permanent storage.

Microfilm

Microfilm was a storage process where documents were photographed onto very long rolls of narrow film stock. When this system was popular, it was used to reduced storage space and costs. It has been reported that a savings of up ninety-eight per cent of hardcopy storage can be saved using this method.

APPENDIX B
DOCUMENT REFERENCE STAMP EXAMPLE

Folder No.: ....

Heading: ....

Subheading: ....

Date Contents Acquired: ....

Source [i.e., how acquired]: ....

Author: ....

Figure 10—Example of a cataloging stamp.

APPENDIX C
INDEXING PRINCIPLES

INTRODUCTION

These principles are applicable to manual intelligence systems only. If we are using a computerized system, the programming package (for example, Microsoft's *Access*) will have its own indexing rules that will be outlined in its user manual. The rules computerized database management systems use may not be subject to alteration by the user unless you are a software developer or "power user."

Step One

The first step in indexing is to divide headings, titles, names and so on into *units*. For example, if we look at the name *Vladimir Putin*, the first unit is "Vladimir" and the second is "Putin." In the heading *Federal Security Service*, the first is "Federal," the second "Security," and the third "Service." If we had longer headings or titles, then each additional word would become a new unit.

Unit One	Unit Two	Unit Three	Unit Four
Vladimir	Putin		
Leningrad	State	University	
Crimea	Annexation		
Federal	Security	Service	
Communist	East	German	Government

Figure 11—"Units" explained.

Step Two

The rule of "nothing comes before something" applies when indexing headings, titles, names, and so on. So, in the following examples, we see that:

DeJay, L. [nothing]

comes before,

DeJay, Lucian M. [nothing]

which comes before,

DeJay, Lucian Milhous

also,

DeJay [nothing], Lucian

comes before,

DeJayne, Lucian

Step Three

Headings prefixed by "Mac" and "Mc." Convention treats both prefixes as "Mac." The only exception is where units have the same suffix, then "Mac" will precede "Mc."

MacLeod	Sally	W.

comes before,

McLeod	Sally	W.

however,

McLennon	Sally	W.

comes before,

MacLeod	Sally	W.

Step Four

Headings beginning "St" and "Saint" are pronounced "saint", and as such, they are indexed as they are sound rather than the way they are spelt.

For example,

St Andrews Hotel

comes before,

Saint John Hospital

Step Five

Headings that have names with other prefixes are indexed as they are spelt.

So,

D'Ettorre Financial Services

comes before,

DeJay, Lucien

Step Six

Hyphenated names in headings are treated as if the name is one.

Barr [nothing]

comes before,

Barr-Smith

which comes before,

Barr-Watts

which comes before,

Barry Investment Bank

Step Seven

Names in headings which contain formal titles, such as Sir, Dr, Captain, Chief, and so on are indexed without consideration to the title.

Marino (Dr), Chiara

Rossi (Dr), Bella.

Step Eight

When all else fails, and you are confronted with a particularly difficult name, you can always refer to the *White Pages* online. No doubt the name that is causing confusion has presented the same problem for the indexers of the telephone book. See how they addressed it and adopt their solution.

APPENDIX D
SAMPLE INFORMATION REPORT FORM

Information from: ……………………………………..

Position: …………………………………………

Location: ………………………………………...

Reported to: ……………………………………..

Date & Time: ……………………………………

Suggested heading: …………………………………..

Suggested subheading: ………………………………

Summary: ……………………………………………

………………………………………………………..

………………………………………………………..

Information: …………………………………………

………………………………………………………..

………………………………………………………..

………………………………………………………..

………………………………………………………..

………………………………………………………..

………………………………………………………..

Signature: ……………………………………………

APPENDIX E
KEYWORDING

Keywording is an extension of subject filing. Below is an example relating to environmental offenses. For a detailed discussion of keywording, see Chapter 4—"Thesaurus," Chapter 5—"How to Create a Thesaurus."

Environmental Offenses

Used for Pollution

Related terms
  Corporate Crime
  Corporate Criminal Liability
  Environmental Laws
  Urban Planning

Figure 12—Example of keywording.

So, under "Pollution" we would place the following alert, "Use Environmental Offenses." And under "Corporate Criminal Liability," related terms could include, "Bribery," "Environmental Laws," "Environmental Offenses," and "White Collar Crimes."

There are two other terms used in a hierarchical thesaurus; these are, narrower terms, and broader terms. But for our purposes (i.e., small intelligence systems) we will not use them. If you ever need to design a large intelligence system, then the US National Criminal Justice Reference Service's thesaurus (Chapter 5), is a good reference work to assist your design work.

ABOUT THE AUTHOR

Dr Henry W. Prunckun is a former Australian government intelligence officer and freelance private investigator who spent much of his career in various operational fields, including security, investigation, and counterterrorism. He also served for over a decade as a research criminologist at Charles Sturt University, Sydney, specializing in the study of transnational crime—espionage, terrorism, drugs and arms trafficking, and cyber-crime.

INDEX

admiralty ratings, 13, 19

Big Brother, 1

Boolean search, 37

data: defined, 36; preliminary analysis of, 18–19; raw, 6, 23, 39; retrieval, 16–17; storage, 16–17

database: commercial applications, 37–38; data, 36; field, 37; file, 37; non-relational, 38; record, 37; relational, 38; template, 37

Dewey Decimal System, 33, 34

documents: continuous filing of, 28–29; purging of, 19–20; reference stamp, 48; tracking, 45–46; warehousing of, 16

equipment: filing, 47

filing: continuous, 28–29; equipment, 47; traditional systems, 27–28; versus indexing, 26–27

indexing: alphabetical, 30–31; cross referencing, 44–45; dead cards, 46fn58; entities, 43–44; geographical, 32–33; keywording, 53; numeric, 31–32; principles, 49–51; rotational, 33–34; subject, 33; systems, 29–35; titling, 29; ultimate, 34–35; versus filing, 26–27.

See also keywords, thesaurus

information: analysis of, 14; collation, 12–13; collection, 7–11; defined, 36; evaluation of, 11; raw, 6, 23, 39; sample report form, 52

intelligence: as knowledge, 4–6; as a process, 6–7; computerized system, 35–38; creating a system, 23–26, 39–40; defined, 2–3; dissemination of, 14–15; manual system, 26–35; typology of, 8–11; versus information, 3

keywords: as a form of subject filing, 53; assigning, 12, 53; defined, 41; example of, 53; in context, 16. *See also* thesaurus, indexing

metadata, 17

purging, 12fn18, 19–20; criteria, 20–21

quality control, 18fn18, 18–19, 21, 36

Soundex, 21–22, 22fn36

Sun Tzu, 1, 23fn37

thesaurus, 33, 33fn44, 40–41; creating, 41–45. *See also* indexing, keywords

US National Criminal Justice Reference Service, 41, 53